AWFULLY ANCIENT

Gory Gladiators,
Savage Centurions
and Caesar's Sticky End

A menacing
history of the
unruly Romans!

First published in paperback in 2016 by Wayland
Copyright © Wayland 2016

Wayland
An imprint of
Hachette Children's Group
Part of Hodder & Stoughton
Carmelite House
50 Victoria Embankment
London EC4Y 0DZ

MIX
Paper from responsible sources
FSC® C104740

Senior editor: Julia Adams
Illustrator: Tom Morgan-Jones
Designer: Rocket Design (East Anglia) Ltd

Dewey classification: 937-dc23

ISBN 978 0 7502 9007 4
Library e-book ISBN 978 0 7502 9369 3

Printed in China
10 9 8 7 6 5 4 3 2 1

An Hachette UK company
www.hachette.co.uk
www.hachettechildrens.co.uk

This guy came to a sticky end. Find out more on page 6.

Can you guess what's in this bag? Turn to page 12 for a full explanation.

What's this famous American icon doing in a book about the Romans? Turn to page 25 to find out!

Contents

What do gladiators, centurions and Julius Caesar have in common? Easy! They were ALL Romans. And they all had a pretty tough time of it too, with oodles of blood and gore and horribly nasty deaths.

Who were the Romans?

Rome is now the capital of Italy. But 2000 years ago, it was at the very heart of a huge — and hugely powerful — republic, which grew to become an even bigger — and even more powerful — empire. The Roman Empire surrounded the Mediterranean Sea. At its height, during the second century CE, it covered 6.5 million square kilometres, which is about the same size as Russia today. All citizens and soldiers of the Roman Empire were known as Romans.

What did the Romans do?

The Romans didn't just conquer a huge empire. They built magnificent aqueducts, bridges and roads. They improved public health by supplying fresh water and taking dirty water away again. They had central heating and toilets. The Roman army even used some of the earliest hospitals. But the Romans had a dark side, too. And as you'll find out in the rest of this book, that was MUCH more bloodthirsty...

The myth versus the truth

Rome – the myth

The Romans believed that in 783 BCE, twin boys called Romulus and Remus were thrown into the River Tiber by their wicked uncle. BOO! But they were washed ashore on an island in the middle of the River Tiber. HURRAY! Then a passing wolf found the boys and took care of them until they were grown up. AWWW.

So what does this have to do with Rome...?

Thirty years later, Mars – the god of war – told Romulus and Remus to build a city in the exact spot where the wolf had found them. But the twins couldn't agree where that was. They fought. Remus was killed. And the city was named Rome after Romulus, the winner.

Rome – the truth

What actually happened was that Rome began as a small village on the banks of the River Tiber. Then the village grew larger. But that wasn't anywhere near as exciting as the story of Romulus and Remus, which is perhaps why the myth was made up in the first place.

Which version do YOU prefer?

Fascinating fact
Rome has only been the capital of Italy since 1871.

The Romans built some awesome (but boring) roads.

M–IV
NAPLES

Introducing... Julius Caesar!

Caeser was a great leader, but he got a bit too big for his own boots!

Julius Caesar was perhaps the most famous Roman ever. Born in 100 BCE into one of Rome's most important families, he quickly worked his way up the political ladder of the Roman Republic. But how far could he go?

The great governor

Roman Gaul was an area of Europe that included what are now France and Luxembourg as well as parts of Switzerland and Germany. But Roman Gaul wasn't a very stable place. Some tribes were threatening to fight back against Roman rule. So when Caesar was made governor of Roman Gaul in 60 BCE, he attacked! And he won. By the time Caesar had been governor for eight years, all of modern France and Belgium were part of the Roman Republic. Plus, now that the Romans had conquered northern France, they would be able to reach Britain more easily. And that's exactly where Caesar went. Twice. He didn't conquer Britain, but he did find out a lot of information that came in useful when the Romans went to finish off the job in 43 CE.

The daring and dastardly dictactor

After his success in Roman Gaul, Caesar was ordered back to Rome. He obeyed, but he took his army with him and attacked the Roman leader, Pompey. Caesar won, which meant that he was now the leader

Tea time, Margaret!

This may be an easy attack...

of the Roman Republic. But he went further and made himself a dictator, too. No one else could rule Rome... until he died.

The sticky end

Caesar passed a number of laws and reforms, including inventing his own calendar. He even had a month named after him — July. But he'd upset a lot of people in his quest for power, and a group of them got together and hatched a deadly plan.

The plotters got their chance on 15 March 44 BCE, the day also known as the Ides of March. As Caesar was on the way to the Senate, Rome's parliament, he was surrounded by 60 of his enemies, armed with knives. It was all over for the Roman leader.

A LOOK BACK IN TIME
Whodunnit?

Caesar's autopsy report says that he probably died because of blood loss, due to multiple stab wounds. Whodunnit? They ALL did.

Now hang on, chaps!

It's said that Caesar suffered 23 stab wounds.

Extra-evil emperors

Soon after Julius Caesar died, the Roman Republic became an Empire, which meant that an emperor was in charge of government, rather than a sole leader. Roman emperors were just like kings and queens used to be. They either inherited power or they seized it! While some ruled in a fair and reasonable way, some emperors were very nasty indeed. Did they have sticky ends too? Read on to find out...

Caligula (ruled 37–41 CE)

Emperor Caligula squeezed an awful lot into his four-year reign. He dug up Alexander the Great's body, so that he could wear the Greek king's armour. He gave Incitatus — not a person, but his favourite horse — a job in the government. And once, while watching gladiators fight, he decided that the show was dull, so he ordered a few rows of the audience to be thrown into the arena to be gobbled up by wild beasts. It's not surprising that his death was as violent as his life. Caligula was stabbed by a bunch of assassins, just like Caesar.

Nero (ruled 54–68 CE)

Emperor Nero poisoned his stepbrother and executed his mother and his wife, before kicking his next wife to death. He was also blamed for setting the city of Rome on fire. At last, the Romans had had enough and they revolted. Fearing that he was about to be killed in a really

We're certain Caligula's horse made some valuable contributions to the running of the empire...

nasty way, Nero asked one of his own servants to finish him off instead.

Domitian (ruled 81–96 CE)

Emperor Domitian executed so many wealthy citizens and important politicians that he made many, many enemies. In the end, they got together and, you've guessed it, stabbed him to death.

Caracalla (ruled 198–217 CE)

When the citizens of Alexandria put on a play making fun of Emperor Caracalla, he was NOT amused! He travelled to the city with an army, invited them into the main square and slaughtered them — some say as many as 20,000 were killed. He was murdered by one of his own bodyguards.

A LOOK BACK IN TIME

Purple peril!

Purple clothes were coloured using a dye made from murex seashells. To make sure that the colour remained VERY exclusive, Emperor Nero introduced a law to ban anyone else but an emperor from wearing it. It was a crime punishable by death. (Though normal citizens probably couldn't afford purple dye anyway, because it was extremely expensive.)

Inside the Roman Army

Taking sides

Telling the difference between legionaries and centurions was easy. A legionary wore his sword on the right, while a centurion wore it on the left. (A centurion also wore a fancier helmet that was black and white.)

A Roman leader was nothing without his army. Tough and well-disciplined, Roman soldiers conquered a vast empire. But the army wasn't just a massive group of soldiers. Troops were organised into smaller groups like this...

Legions

There were around 30 legions in the Roman army. In each legion there were usually about 4,800 soldiers, but sometimes as many as 5,400.

Cohorts

There were ten cohorts in each legion and in each cohort there were about 480 soldiers.

Centuries

In each cohort there were six centuries. With a name like century, which is also the name for 100 years, you might think that there were 100 soldiers in each, but it was actually 80.

Legionaries

The soldiers in a century were called legionaries. They were trained hard to make sure that they did their job properly. They marched (carrying ALL their kit), they practised using their weapons and if they did anything wrong, they were punished. And they did this for 25 YEARS, because that's how long a soldier signed up for. Luckily, if a legionary was still alive after 20 years, the last five years in the army weren't quite such hard work. Er, phew.

A Roman spear, or pilum. It was a massive two metres long and could smash right through a shield, stabbing the soldier behind – arghh!

A Roman sword, or gladius. Best avoid anyone brandishing one of these...

Situation vacant
ROMAN CENTURION

Fancy going for this?

Applicants must:

- be able to read and write;
- have several years' experience in the Roman army;
- have friends in high places who are prepared to say how terrific they are;
- be at least 30 years old;
- be big and strong and good at throwing things such as spears and javelins;
- be pretty handy with a sword and a shield;
- be good at following orders;
- be REALLY good at making sure the soldiers under their command are well-behaved, supremely fit, clean and have super-shiny weapons;
- be prepared to dish out the harshest punishments ever invented if their century does ANYTHING wrong.

Legionaries marched carrying their ENTIRE kit. It was a bit of a heavy load.

Centurions

The officer in charge of a century was called a centurion, while a senior centurion commanded a cohort. But these weren't just any old soldiers. Take a look at the job description above to see just how tricky it was to become one of the most feared soldiers in the Roman army.

Dreadful Discipline

Romans didn't faff about with the 'naughty step'.

Arghh!

With so many soldiers to keep in order, the Romans were hot on discipline. So the punishments for misbehaving were VERY harsh indeed.

Punishing the soldiers

There were different punishments for different crimes. Some were worse than others, but all were pretty scary. If a legionary stepped out of line in the Roman army, here's what happened to them.

① Desertion

If found guilty, the soldier would be stoned or beaten to death with clubs by his fellow soldiers.

② Disobeying an order

The punishment was flogging, sometimes as many as 200 lashes of the whip. This would be carried out in front of the legion.

③ Theft

The soldier would be tied up in a sack of snakes and thrown into the river. Or strangled. To be honest, neither option was much fun.

④ Being a coward

If the legion was cowardly in battle, the punishment was decimation, which is the Latin way of saying that a tenth is removed. In this case, a tenth of the soldiers was removed in a particularly nasty way. First, they were divided into groups of 10, then they drew lots and one unlucky soldier from each group was chosen. Then he was beaten to death by the other nine.

Oh, goody, goody, look chaps, I've won... haven't I?

You could get a lot more than you bargained for by winning the 'decimation' tombola!

A LOOK BACK IN TIME

Punishing the enemy

If you thought that the Romans treated their own soldiers badly, it'll come as no surprise that they treated their enemies even worse...

The Spartacus Rebellion (73–71 BC)

When Spartacus – the gladiator who famously led a slave rebellion – was defeated by the Roman general Crassus, the countryside was scoured for survivors. Six thousand slaves were captured and then they were crucified on crosses dotted all along the 212 km Appian Way – a Roman road between Rome and Capua. It was a reminder to everyone else that attacking Rome was NOT a good idea.

Vercingetorix, the leader of the Gauls who had fought against Caesar, was captured in 52 CE, after the Battle of Alesia. But the Romans didn't inflict terrible punishment straight away. Vercingetorix was imprisoned for five years. Then he was paraded through Rome. And finally he was garrotted in an underground prison.

Law and Order

Forgers are my favourites.

It wasn't just armies and enemies that the Romans had to keep in order. They had to make sure all their citizens behaved, too. And this was pretty tricky without an actual police force.

Emergency!

Roman laws only dealt with serious crimes, such as murder or grave injury. There were no emergency services to deal with everyday problems such as crime and fire. Then, in 6 CE, Emperor Augustus set up a group of men called vigiles, who worked as police officers and fire fighters. They were divided into cohorts and then centuries, each commanded by a centurion, just like the Roman army.

Vigiles were the watchmen of the city. They stayed alert for any disturbances, patrolling day and night, on the lookout for burglars and runaway slaves. They stopped riots and kept order on the streets. And they put out fires, too, which were a big problem in overcrowded Rome.

Meanwhile, the emperor himself was perfectly safe. He had bodyguards, called the Praetorian Guard, to look after him.

Guilty!

What happened if a person was caught doing something wrong? It depended on the crime. But Romans weren't known for their forgiveness. Here are a few of the terrible punishments they dished out.

TRAITORS were beheaded. Heads went one way (into the sewers) and bodies another (into the River Tiber).

Right, you're coming with me... when I've put this fire out.

FORGERS were fed to wild beasts in an arena. This wasn't just punishment — it was entertainment for crowds of Romans, too!

THIEVES were punished in lots of different ways. If they stole crops, they were strangled. If they stole food, they were sent to work in a mine. If they stole a deer, they were wrapped in the deerskin and chased by dogs.

A LOOK BACK IN TIME
Given the sack

To a Roman, patricide — killing your own father — was the most terrible of all crimes. If found guilty, you would be whipped, then sewn into a leather sack. But you wouldn't have to worry about being lonely, because a dog, a rooster, a snake and a monkey would be put in there, too. And then the sack would be thrown into the River Tiber. Splosh!

15

Slaving Away

> Would you mind carrying me to the bathroom, guys?

Without slaves, wealthy Romans would have had much tougher lives. Slaves did all the jobs that Romans didn't want to do. Usually captured in battle, they were sold at slave markets or born to other slaves. Sometimes, if they were short of cash, Romans sold their eldest children into slavery. And unless they bought their freedom or were freed by their masters, once someone was a slave, they were a slave for life.

How much?!

The price of a slave depended on their skills. For example, rich Romans liked to show off to their friends by hosting extravagant banquets, so they needed top chefs. This meant that slaves who could cook were very expensive.

Teachers and doctors fetched a high price, too. Meanwhile, unskilled slaves were cheap, because there were more of them on the market. They might work as miners — a dangerous job in Roman times. Life expectancy was horribly short.

As for the average slave's price tag, they cost less than a horse or a cow.

Ludicrous laws

Slaves were the property of their owners, which meant that they did not have the same rights as Roman citizens. One truly silly law stated that if a slave appeared in court, their word would not be believed unless they had been tortured. The Romans thought that a slave must be so loyal to their master that there was no way they could reveal secrets about them without being tortured first. Unbelievably, it was also completely legal to kill a slave if they escaped.

A LOOK BACK IN TIME

Skilled staff

Romans thought that if they didn't have any slaves, everyone else would think they were REALLY poor. Some owned hundreds of slaves. A rich Roman might take three slaves with them just to go to the baths. And slaves did just about every other job that had ever been invented. Here are just a few...

Blacksmith
Carpenter
Carrying their master around in a litter
Cleaner
Construction worker
Cook

Dresser
Farm worker
Gardener
Gladiator
Hairdresser
Launderer
Miner

Shopkeeper
Sommelier
Torch bearer
Waiter
And many, many more.

Roman Gods and Godesses

Juno
Queen of the gods.
She was like Wonder Woman!

Neptune
God of the sea,
carried a trident.

The Romans believed that their gods had the same feelings and needs as normal people. It's just that they had special powers, too, a bit like superheroes. Roman mythology is the collection of stories — or myths — told about the Roman gods, who were all part of one big family.

Ye gods!

Each god or goddess had their own job to do; they were all responsible for different places, things or people. The Romans prayed to whichever god or goddess could help them with a particular problem. And when they prayed, they usually made a sacrifice to that god or goddess, too.

Romans offered everything from milk, cheese and wine to live animals. VERY rarely, they sacrificed people, too. Yikes.

Jupiter — the king of the gods. He was also the god of the sky. When he was angry, he hurled thunderbolts. ZAP!

Juno — the queen of the gods. She was also the goddess of women.

Neptune — the god of the sea. If he was happy, the sea was calm; if he was angry, there were huge waves. He was shown holding a trident — a three-pronged spear.

Pluto — the god of the underworld. This is where

the Romans believed that a person's spirit went after death.

Mars — the god of war. He was popular with the Roman army and so important that the month of March was named after him.

Venus — the goddess of love. Julius Caesar said that she was actually one of his ancestors!

Mercury — the messenger of the gods. He wore winged shoes and a winged hat, so he could travel more swiftly.

Minerva — the goddess of wisdom. She was very popular in Rome. Minerva's festival in March was five days long.

Apollo — the god of the sun. He must have been kept very busy, because he was also the god of light, truth, prophecy, healing, plague, music, poetry and agriculture. Wow.

Diana — the goddess of the moon. She was also linked to hunting and could talk to animals.

Mercury
Messenger of the gods (with cool shoes!)

Jupiter
Thunderbolt-chucking king of the gods.

What's in a name?
The Romans gods and the Greek gods were very similar to each other – they just had different names. For example, the king of the gods was called Jupiter in ancient Rome, while he was known as Zeus in ancient Greece.

Peacock Brains and Flamingo Tongues

Disguising the rank taste of mouldy food was easy. Just cover it with a positively fowl tasting sauce.

What a Roman ate depended on how wealthy they were. While the poor might eat a plain meal of vegetables and porridge, rich Romans could be enjoying many different courses of fancy food.

Fabulous feasts

Rich Romans liked to eat — a lot. And they liked to show off, too. So a banquet was the perfect way to satisfy their appetites and impress their friends at the same time. They feasted on wild boar, venison, wild goat, hare, mutton, sows' udders, peacock brains, flamingo tongues, ostriches, thrushes, peacocks, snails, all sorts of fish, and oysters. And stuffed dormice, of course. This speciality was banned for a time, but the Romans ate it anyway.

Super sauce

Because it could be difficult to stop meat and fish going rotten in the heat, Roman cooks also made a cooking sauce called garum to pour over everything. It disguised the smell and taste of mouldy food beautifully. If you'd like to make your own garum, simply marinate fish guts in salty water for a few weeks. Delicious! (Probably.)

Don't forget the veg!

The Romans were huge fans of fish and meat, but that didn't mean they missed out on fruit and vegetables. They loved olives and pears, quinces and apples. And they adored cabbage and cauliflower, onions and courgettes.

Roman takeaways

If there wasn't the time — or the money — to prepare a huge feast, there was fast food instead. Fritters and pasties were sold from stands. These were especially popular with poorer Romans.

Even the Romans had fast food...

Peacock

Dormouse

Oysters

Udders

Ribs

Goat

Wild Boar

Snails

Get out of here!

Have you ever heard of a vomitorium? You may think it sounds just like the sort of place where Romans might go to vomit. If so, think again. Romans headed for the vomitorium not when they were feeling sick, but when they wanted to make a swift exit. Vomitoria — the word for more than one vomitorium — were actually passages in an amphitheatre. They allowed Romans to make a quick exit after a performance, not throw up.

Fish fancies

Roman foodies loved to eat licker fish. This creature lived in the River Tiber and fed on sewage. Mmm...

Ewww!

Flushed with Success!

Ahem!

Wee was used to bleach wool and cloth.

The Romans knew that if their citizens and soldiers were clean, they were much more likely to be healthy and fit, too. So they built the world's first public-health system, with proper plumbing and superb sewers. Amazing aqueducts carried fresh water to towns, where people could wash in public baths and go to the toilet in comfort. Afterwards, the dirty water and sewage was whisked away.

Roman loos

Toilets were friendly places, with rows of open seats that sat up to 60 people at a time. Here, Romans could chat while they, um, went. But there was one thing they didn't have... toilet paper. Instead, it's said that Romans wiped their bottoms with a sponge on a stick. And they shared that sponge. Yuck.

Not all toilets were communal. The very wealthiest Romans had a toilet in their own home. And if poorer Romans couldn't be bothered to trek all the way to the public toilets, they just filled up a pot at home and threw the contents out of the nearest window!

Roman baths

As well as sharing toilets, the Romans shared baths, too. But they didn't wash in there. Oh no. Before Romans got anywhere near water, they sat in a hot, steamy room, which made them sweat horribly. And then, because the sweating made their pores open so the dirt could ooze out, they scraped themselves clean with a metal tool. Only then could they get into the baths — a choice of warm or cold — with their friends.

A LOOK BACK IN TIME

Roman recycling

The Romans scored top marks for water conservation. Instead of just letting it drain away, they used the dirty water from public baths to flush the toilets.

Even wee was recycled. Romans tiddled into big pots that stood on street corners and the contents were used by fullers. These were people whose job it was to clean and prepare cloth (often wool) so that it could be made into clothes. And it just so happens that wee is very good at bleaching cloth.

Fashion NOT Allowed

Roman male citizens didn't have to waste time deciding what to wear. The choice was made for them; it was the law that they had to wear a toga. It showed that they were important members of Roman society. And it was also a way of making sure that people didn't spend too much money on the latest fashions.

Terrific togas

The toga was made from a long piece of woollen cloth that was draped round the body and then over one arm. Underneath, men wore a linen tunic. But not all togas were white. Dark togas were worn by those in mourning, while off-white togas with a purple border were worn by magistrates and brilliant white togas were worn by the senators.

Romans DEFINITELY didn't do tie-dye.

Smashing stolas

After the second century BCE, the Romans decided that women citizens should wear stolas instead of togas. The stola was made of two rectangular pieces of linen that were buttoned together. As well as the stola, a shawl could be worn as a coat or draped over the arm.

Super-stola
If you want to see a stola, look no further than New York Harbor in the USA. The Statue of Liberty (the Roman goddess of freedom, named Libertas) is wearing one!

At 46 metres high, this is probably the world's largest stola!

A LOOK BACK IN TIME

Roman hairdressing

A list of simply super services were available to make the Roman citizen look REALLY great...

1. Going bald?
Mix together mice, horse teeth and bear fat. Rub it on. If THAT doesn't work, simply pop a laurel wreath on your head, like Julius Caesar did.

2. Going grey?
Just combine oil with earthworm ashes and colour your hair with the mixture. Out of stock? Go for goat fat and beechwood ashes instead.

3. How about a fancy wig?
You're guaranteed to look and feel extra-special in a wig made from one of Rome's enemy's REAL hair!

Glorious and Gory Gladiators

Oh, it was nothing really.

A gladiator was a celebrity and a sporting superstar rolled into one. Most of them were slaves, though some Roman citizens volunteered, too. If they impressed spectators enough by the way they fought other gladiators and criminals in an arena, they could become very famous indeed.

Gladiator school

This wasn't like any school you might have been to. For a start, it was really a prison. The trainee warriors slept in cells and they perfected their skills in an arena inside the high walls. The only time they were allowed outside was to practise in the nearest amphitheatre.

It wasn't a gladiator's job to finish off the opposition as quickly as possible. It was their job to fight in a way that would thrill and entertain the crowds that flocked to see them. So this is what they learned to do. It was also a good idea to try to stay alive in the arena. After all, it took so long and cost so much to train a gladiator that those in charge wanted to get their money's worth out of them.

Into the arena...

Gladiators performed in huge, circular or oval-shaped arenas. A display was free to watch, because emperors and wealthy Romans footed the bill.

Bestiarii were men who fought wild animals, such as bears, lions, leopards or rhinoceroses. This was much more dangerous than being a gladiator.

... and on with the show!

Gladiators could fight with whatever they liked — maybe a shield, a sword, a dagger, a hammer or a trident — and they wore armour, too. If they won, they were paid. If they survived for five years, they were freed! But if they fought against another gladiator and died, they were expected to do it in style, by grabbing the thigh of the winner, who would then stab them in the neck.

A LOOK BACK IN TIME
Inside the Colosseum

Rome's Colosseum was a top spot for gladiatorial contests. Built nearly 2000 years ago, it was the biggest amphitheatre in the entire Roman Empire, with enough room for 50,000 spectators inside. There was sand on the floor to soak up blood, while trap doors led to the cages where men and animals waited until it was their turn to fight.

Erm... I thought we were meant to be creative?

Some gladiators preferred to play it safe...

Tasty treatment
Some Roman physicians recommended drinking gladiators' blood to cure epilepsy.

The End of an Empire

Odoacer

So if Roman emperors were so good at conquering other countries, keeping control of their own citizens and making sure that most people — except the slaves, of course — had a fabulous time, why did the Roman Empire ever end?

Why?!

The Roman Empire fell in 476 CE, when the last-ever emperor, Romulus Augustus, was thrown out of power by a Germanic chieftan called Odoacer. But this wasn't the only reason why the empire fizzled out. The truth is that things hadn't been looking good for the Romans for a while because of a whole load of other problems. And there are now hundreds of ideas that try to explain why such a great civilisation lost its power. Here are just a few...

● Barbarians invaded not just once but MANY times. In 410 CE, they even attacked the city of Rome — and won!

● The Romans had spent a lot of money on wars and having fun, and now they were running out of cash. Not even raising taxes helped, because the wealthy Romans ran away to avoid paying them.

● Now that the Romans weren't invading new countries, they weren't capturing enemies to sell as slaves and were running out of those, too.

● Civil wars, corruption and plague have also been blamed.

Poisoned population?
Some historians think that because the Romans used so much lead in their aqueducts and water pipes and cooking pots – it was even an ingredient in food – the Roman population was being slowly poisoned.

Romulus Augustus

Oi, come back here!

Not-so-ancient Rome

If you check out photos of modern Rome – or are lucky enough to visit the Italian capital yourself – you really CAN look back in time. This is because some of the amazing structures that the mighty Romans built are still there. They may be in ruins, but with a little imagination you just might be able to experience what it was like to be part of one of the greatest ancient civilisations ever. Go on, try.

❀ The Roman Forum was a space in the middle of Rome that was once surrounded by government buildings and temples. They are now magnificent and well-preserved ruins.

❀ The Circus Maximus was a chariot race track. The track is gone, but its grassy outline remains.

❀ The Colosseum was the largest amphitheatre in the Roman Empire. It's mostly still there!

Many wealthy Romans managed to avoid paying taxes...

Chariot racing was hugely popular in ancient Rome.

29

Glossary

aqueduct – an ancient Roman structure that brought fresh water into towns and cities

arena – a space where the gladiators fought in front of spectators

Caesar, Julius – famous Roman general and dictator who was assassinated; ruled 49–44 BCE

Caligula – Roman emperor, ruled 37–41 CE

Caracalla – Roman emperor, ruled 198–217 CE

decimation – execution of every tenth man in the legion for mutiny

Domitian – Roman emperor, ruled 81–96 CE

emperor – ruler of the Roman Empire

garrotted – strangled

garum – a fish sauce that was made to disguise the smell and taste of rotten food

gladiator – trained professional fighter

legionary – Roman soldier

Mars – the Roman god of war

Nero – Roman emperor, ruled 54–68 CE

Rome – the capital of the Roman Empire

Romulus and Remus – the mythical founders of Rome

senators – Roman politicians who helped run the empire

Spartacus – the leader of a slave rebellion

stola – a garment worn by Roman women

Tarpeian Rock – a steep cliff overlooking the Roman Forum where Roman traitors were executed

Tiber – the river that flows through Rome

toga – long cloth that was wrapped around the body over a tunic; it was worn by men in ancient Rome

vigiles – the Roman police force who were responsible for fighting crime and putting out fires in ancient Rome

More information

Places to visit

Hadrian's Wall, northern England
Hadrian's Wall country stretches across the north of England from the west Cumbrian Roman coastal defences at Ravenglass to South Shields on the River Tyne. Fabulous forts to visit are at Vindolanda, Housesteads and Chesters. www.english-heritage.org.uk/daysout/hadrianswall

National Roman Legion Museum, Newport
This museum vividly portrays the story of the conquest and occupation of Wales by the Romans. www.museumwales.ac.uk/roman

British Museum, London
The Department of Greece and Rome at the British Museum has one of the most comprehensive collections of antiquities from the classical world, with over 100,000 objects. www.britishmuseum.org

National Museum of Scotland, Edinburgh
The Early People gallery of the National Museum of Scotland contains a wealth of material that tells us the story of the Romans in Scotland. www.nms.ac.uk/national-museum-of-scotland

Websites

www.historylearningsite.co.uk
Roman Education – History Learning Site

www.bbc.co.uk/schools/primaryhistory/romans
A History of Ancient Rome on the website of the BBC

Books

Truth or Busted: Warm Gladiator Blood Was Used As Medicine! The Fact or Fiction Behind Romans by Peter Hepplewhite, Wayland (2014)

What They Don't Tell You About Romans in Britain by Bob Fowke, Wayland (2013)

Barmy Biogs: Dastardly Dictators, Rulers and other Loony Leaders by Paul Harrison, Wayland (2013)

Index